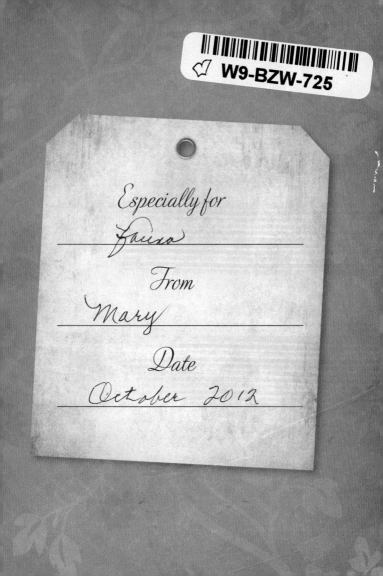

Especially for
Laura

From
Mary

Date
October 2012

A Touch
of Joy

Helen Steiner Rice

BARBOUR
PUBLISHING

Published by Barbour Publishing, Inc., P.O. Box 719, Uhrichsville, Ohio 44683
www.barbourbooks.com

Cover design: Greg Jackson, Thinkpen Design

Our mission is to publish and distribute inspirational products offering exceptional value and biblical encouragement to the masses.

Member of the
Evangelical Christian
Publishers Association

Printed in the United States of America.

Contents

In Nature

You will live in joy and peace.
The mountains and hills will burst into song,
and the trees of the field will clap their hands!

Isaiah 55:12 NLT

God's gifts are all around you, dear friend.
Picture your heavenly Father fashioning each
flower, each tree, each star, each bird on the
wing. Can you see Him smiling as He creates
these beautiful gifts for His children? Look
around you—really look. See what He has done.
Then lift up your hands and your voice. Let Him
see and hear that you appreciate His handiwork.
Let Him see what joy His gifts have brought to
your life.

Dear Yuenne,

I don't know you well yet but I
feel a kindred spirit. Even though I'm dying here
for,) I almost lost him numerous times
between 2008 and now. He seems to be dying too.
We wish we'd been all set up for the numerous
times with no reason nor to be
getting nerdy for his "somegoing" and finally I
couldn't take every him Totally be all exerts
here April 1st. He's done so well and experts
say his heart so weak etc. For to go
on but I wanted you to know it's purely itchy
but to give him a big hearty a justice to this
because I was beyond myself. I found you to
this little book and I will send in a very
day. I'm really in this out really there out.
Congrats me ___ I will send what you are great.
Through and pls Bye thx you

He strength a courage.
I see it in you. xo

Each time you look up in the sky
Or watch the fluffy clouds drift by,
Or feel the sunshine
    warm and bright,
Or watch the dark night
    turn to light,
Or hear a bluebird sweetly sing,
Or see the winter turn to spring,
Or touch a leaf or see a tree,
It's all God whispering,
    "This is Me. . ."

Through all of creation with
  symphonic splendor
God speaks with a voice
  that is gentle and tender.
And the birds in the trees
  and the flowers of spring
All join in proclaiming
  this heavenly King.

Though you have not seen him, you love him; and even though you do not see him now, you believe in him and are filled with an inexpressible and glorious joy.

1 Peter 1:8

He's the stars in the heaven,
  a smile on some face,
A leaf on a tree or a rose in a vase.
He's winter and autumn
  and summer and spring,
In short, God is every real
  and wonderful thing.

You ask me how I know it's true
  that there is a living God...
A God who rules the universe—
  the sky, the sea, the sod—
A God who hangs the sun out
  slowly with the break of day
And gently takes the stars in
  and puts the night away.
What better answers are there
  to prove His holy being
Than the wonders all around us
  that are ours just for the seeing?

Apple blossoms bursting wide
   now beautify the tree
And make a springtime picture
   that is beautiful to see.
As the flowering branches
   depend upon the tree
To nourish and fulfill them
   till they reach maturity,
We, too, must be dependent
   on our Father up above,
For we are but the branches
   and He's the tree of love.

After the winter comes the spring
To show us again that in everything
There's always a renewal
    divinely planned,
Flawlessly perfect,
    the work of God's hand.

God lives in the beauty
that comes with spring—
The colorful flowers,
the birds that sing—
And He lives in people
as kind as you,
And He lives in all the
nice things you do.

April comes with cheeks a-glowing
Silver streams are all a-flowing,
Flowers open wide their eyes
In lovely rapturous surprise.
Lilies dream beside the brooks,
Violets in meadow nooks,
And the birds gone wild with glee
Fill the woods with melody.

Flowers sleeping 'neath the snow,
Awakening when the spring winds blow,
Leafless trees so bare before
Gowned in lacy green once more,
Hard, unyielding, frozen sod
Now softly carpeted by God;
Still streams melting in the spring,
Rippling over rocks that sing,
Barren, windswept, lonely hills
Turning gold with daffodils—
These miracles are all around,
Within our sight and touch and sound,
As true and wonderful today
As when the stone was rolled away,
Proclaiming to all doubting men
That in God all things live again.

Springtime is a season
   of hope and joy and cheer—
There's beauty all around us
   to see and touch and hear. . .
So no matter how downhearted
   and discouraged we may be,
New hope is born when we behold
   leaves budding on a tree
Or when we see a timid flower
   push through the frozen sod
And open wide in glad surprise
   its petaled eyes to God.

I come to meet You, God,
   and as I linger here
I seem to feel You very near.
A rustling leaf, a rolling slope
Speak to my heart of endless hope.
The sun just rising in the sky,
The waking birdlings as they fly,
The grass all wet with morning dew
Are telling me I just met You.

Gently, thus the day is born
As night gives way to breaking morn,
And once again I've met You, God,
And worshipped on Your holy sod. . .
For who could see the
  dawn break through
Without a glimpse of heaven and You?
For who but God could make the day
And softly put the night away?

I see the dew glisten
   in crystal-like splendor
While God, with a touch that is
   gentle and tender,
Wraps up the night and
   softly tucks it away
And hangs out the sun
   to herald a new day.

Dear God, there are things
  we cannot measure
Like the depths of waves and sea
And the heights of stars in heaven
And the joy You bring to me.

In Faith

Though you have not seen him, you love him;
and even though you do not see him now,
you believe in him and are filled with
an inexpressible and glorious joy.

1 Peter 1:8

Joy—the kind God gives—is a faith thing. As you receive by faith what God has provided for you, your joy grows. As you slip your hand in His and walk in faith, believing that His paths are good, your joy thrives regardless of the circumstances in your life. As you place your burdens, your future, your limitations, your pride, your hopes and fears in His hands, the joy of the Lord will fill every corner of your heart.

Faith to believe when
 the way is rough
And faith to hang on
 when the going is tough
Will never fail to pull us through
And bring us strength
 and comfort, too.

Faith makes it wholly possible
to quietly endure
The violent world around us,
for in God we are secure.

All we really ever need
Is faith as a grain of mustard seed,
For all God asks is that you believe.
For if you do, ye shall receive.

Take heart and meet each minute
with faith in God's great love,
Aware that every day of life
is controlled by God above...
And never dread tomorrow
or what the future brings—
Just pray for strength and courage
and trust God in all things.

"For I know the plans I have for you,"
declares the Lord, *"plans to prosper you*
and not to harm you, plans to give
you hope and a future."

Jeremiah 29:11

When the darkness shuts out the light,
We must lean on faith
   to restore our sight,
For there is nothing we need know
If we have faith that wherever we go
God will be there to help us to bear
Our disappointments, pain, and care.

No day is too dark and
   no burden too great
That God in His love
   cannot penetrate…
And to know and believe
   without question or doubt
That no matter what happens
   God is there to help out
Is to hold in your hand
   the golden key
To peace and joy and serenity.

Oh, Father, grant once more to men
A simple, childlike faith again,
Forgetting color, race, and creed
And seeing only
     the heart's deep need. . .
For faith alone can save man's soul
And lead him to a higher goal,
For there's but one
     unfailing course—
We win by faith and not by force.

For with patience to wait
     and faith to endure,
Your life will be blessed
     and your future secure,
For God is but testing
     your faith and your love
Before He appoints you
     to rise far above
All the small things
     that so sorely distress you,
For God's only intention is
     to strengthen and bless you.

It's easy to grow downhearted
   when nothing goes your way.
It's easy to be discouraged when
   you have a troublesome day.
But trouble is only a challenge
   to spur you on to achieve
The best that God has to offer
   if you have the faith to believe.

Faith is a force that is greater than
    knowledge or power or skill,
And the darkest defeat turns to
    triumph if you trust in God's
    wisdom and will,
For faith is a mover of mountains—
    there's nothing man cannot achieve
If he has the courage to try it
    and then has the faith to believe.

Though I cannot find Your hand
To lead me on to the Promised Land,
I still believe with all my being
Your hand is there beyond my seeing.

*"Blessed are those
who have not seen
and yet have believed."*

John 20:29

Nothing is ever too hard to do
If your faith is strong and your
     purpose is true. . .
So never give up, and never stop—
Just journey on to the mountaintop!

In a small child's shining eyes
The faith of all ages lies. . .
And tiny hands and tousled heads
That kneel in prayer by little beds.

In Prayer

This is the confidence we have in approaching God:
that if we ask anything according to his will,
he hears us. And if we know that he hears us—
whatever we ask—we know that we
have what we asked of him.

1 John 5:14–15

Prayer is first and foremost a conversation between two parties—you and Almighty God. Imagine what privilege that affords, for there is no higher court, no ear more ready to listen than His. Bring Him your requests, place them at His feet, and then linger long in His presence. Oh what joy you will experience knowing that He has the power to do the impossible. Go to Him often in prayer. He welcomes you.

It fills me with joy just to
   linger with You,
As my soul You replenish
   and my heart You renew.
So thank You again for
   Your mercy and love
And for making me heir
   to Your kingdom above.

Kneel in prayer in His presence,
   and you'll find no need to speak;
For softly in quiet communion,
   God grants you the peace
   that you seek.

Prayer is so often just words unspoken,

Whispered in tears by a heart that is broken,

For God is already deeply aware

Of the burdens we find too heavy to bear...

And all we need do is seek Him in prayer,

And without a word He will help us to bear

Our trials and troubles,

   our sickness and sorrow,

And show us the way to a brighter tomorrow.

There's no need at all for impressive prayer,

For the minute we seek God

   He's already there.

Whenever we're troubled
and lost in despair,
We have but to seek Him
and ask Him in prayer
To guide and direct us
and help us to bear
Our sickness and sorrow,
our worry and care.

Teach me to do your will,
for you are my God;
may your good Spirit
lead me on level ground.

PSALM 143:10

Though we feel helpless
    and alone when we start,
A prayer is the key that
    opens the heart,
And as the heart opens,
    the dear Lord comes in
And the prayer that we felt
    we could never begin
Is so easy to say,
    for the Lord understands
And He gives us new strength
    by the touch of His hands.

On the wings of prayer
    our burdens take flight
And our load of care
    becomes bearably light
And our heavy hearts
    are lifted above
To be healed by the balm
    of God's wonderful love.

I cannot dwell apart from You—
You would not ask or want me to,
For You have room within Your heart
To make each child of Yours a part
Of You and all Your love and care
If we but come to You in prayer.

My garden beautifies my yard
and adds fragrance to the air...
But it is also my cathedral
and my quiet place of prayer...
So little do we realize
that the glory and the power
Of Him who made the universe
lies hidden in a flower.

Just close your eyes and open your heart
And feel your worries and cares depart,
Just yield yourself to the Father above
And let Him hold you secure in His love.
So when you are tired, discouraged, and blue,
There's always one door that is open to you—
For the heart is a temple when God is there
As we place ourselves in His loving care.

Brighten your day
And lighten your way
And lessen your cares
With daily prayers.
Quiet your mind
And leave tension behind
And find inspiration
In hushed meditation.

How true!

When we seek shelter
   in His wondrous love,
And ask Him to send us
   help from above. . .
Then we find comfort
   and know it is true
That bright, shining hours
   and dark, sad ones, too,
Are part of the plan God
   made for each one,
And all we need pray is,
   "Thy will be done."

To you, O LORD,
I lift up my soul.

PSALM 25:1

Although it sometimes seems to us
   our prayers have not been heard,
God always knows our every need
   without a single word,
And He will not forsake us,
   even though the way is steep.
For always He is near us,
   a tender watch to keep. . .
And in good time He'll answer us,
   and in His love He'll send
Greater things than we have asked
   and blessings without end.

Whenever I am troubled
    and lost in deep despair,
I bundle all my troubles up
    and go to God in prayer…
I know He stilled the tempest
    and calmed the angry sea,
And I humbly ask if, in His love,
    He'll do the same for me…
And then I just keep quiet
    and think only thoughts of peace,
And as I abide in stillness
    my restless murmurings cease.

There is only one place
   and only one Friend
Who is never too busy,
   and you can always depend
On Him to be waiting,
   with arms open wide,
To hear all the troubles
   you came to confide.
For the heavenly Father
   will always be there
When you seek Him and find Him
   at the altar of prayer.

Tavene,

I said a special prayer for you—
    I asked the Lord above
To keep you safely in His care
    and enfold you in His love.
I did not ask for fortune,
    for riches or for fame,
I only asked for blessings
    in the Holy Savior's name—
Blessings to surround you
    in time of trial and stress,
And inner joy to fill your heart
    with peace and happiness. *L. M.*

Prayers are the stairs that lead to
   God, and there's joy
   every step of the way
When we make our pilgrimage to
   Him with love in our hearts
   each day.

"Ask and it will be given to you;
seek and you will find; knock and the
door will be opened to you."

Matthew 7:7

There's no problem too big
    and no question too small—
Just ask God in faith,
    and He'll answer them all—
Not always at once,
    so be patient and wait,
For God never comes too soon
    or too late. . .
So trust in His wisdom
    and believe in His Word,
For no prayer's unanswered
    and no prayer's unheard.

All of our errors and failures that
    we made in the course of the day
Are freely forgiven at nighttime
    when we kneel down
    and earnestly pray,
So seek the Lord in the morning
    and never forget Him at night,
For prayer is an unfailing blessing
    that makes every burden
    seem light.

Let us hold tightly without wavering to the hope we affirm, for God can be trusted to keep his promise.

<small>Hebrews 10:23 nlt</small>

Is it possible to be joyful even in the face of trials and tribulations? It is, dear friend! When your faith is tried, it grows stronger, more mature and resilient, because it allows God to demonstrate His love and His faithfulness to you. These triumphs may not come in the packages you expect, but they are fashioned by God's wisdom and understanding. Rejoice, dear friend, even in your trials.

When you're troubled and
   worried and sick at heart
And your plans are upset
   and your world falls apart,
Remember God's ready
   and waiting to share
The burden you find
   too heavy to bear.

Life can't always be a song—
You have to have trouble to
make you strong,
So whenever you are troubled
and everything goes wrong,
It is just God working in you
to make your spirit strong.

Nothing in life can defeat me,
For as long as this knowledge
    remains,
I can suffer whatever is happening,
For I know God will break
    all the chains
That are binding me tight
    in the darkness
And trying to fill me with fear. . .
For there is no night
    without dawning,
And I know that my morning
    is near.

God never plows in the soul of man
Without intention and purpose
   and plan. . .
So whenever you feel the
   plow's sharp blade
Let not your heart be sorely afraid,
For, like the farmer,
   God chooses a field
From which He expects
   an excellent yield. . .
So rejoice though your heart
   be broken in two—
God seeks to bring forth
   a rich harvest in you.

"I have told you these things,
so that in me you may have peace.
In this world you will have trouble.
But take heart! I have overcome the world."

John 16:33

No one discovers the fullness
   or the greatness of God's love
Unless they have walked in the
   darkness with only a light
   from above. . .
For the failure to endure whatever
   comes is born of sorrow and trials
And strengthened only by discipline
   and nurtured by self-denials;
So be not disheartened by troubles,
   for trials are the building blocks
On which to erect a fortress of faith,
   secure on God's ageless rocks.

He is our Shepherd,
  our Father, our Guide,
And you're never alone
  with the Lord at your side. . .
So may the Great Physician
  attend you,
And may His healing
  completely mend you.

With faith in your heart,
 reach out for God's hand
And accept what He sends,
 though you can't understand...
For our Father in heaven
 always knows what is best,
And if you trust in His wisdom,
 your life will be blessed...
For always remember that
 whatever betide you,
You are never alone,
 for God is beside you.

When life seems empty
and there's no place to go,
When your heart is troubled
and your spirits are low
When friends seem few and nobody cares
There is always God to hear your prayers.
So go to our Father when
troubles assail you,
For His grace is sufficient
and He'll never fail you.

Growing trees are strengthened
when they withstand the storm,
And the sharp cut of a chisel gives
the marble grace and form.
God never hurts us needlessly
and He never wastes our pain,
For every loss He sends to us
is followed by rich gain.

So whenever we are troubled and
   when everything goes wrong,
It is just God working in us
   to make our spirits strong.
We love the sound of laughter
   and the merriment of cheer,
But our hearts would lose their
   tenderness if we never shed a tear. . .
So whenever we are troubled
   and life has lost its song
It's God testing us with burdens
   just to make our spirit strong!

Never dread tomorrow
    or what the future brings
Just pray for strength and courage
    and trust God in all things,
And never grow discouraged—
    be patient and just wait,
For God never comes too early,
    and He never comes too late.

*The L*ORD *is my strength and my shield;*
my heart trusts in him, and I am helped.
My heart leaps for joy and I will give
thanks to him in song.

PSALM 28:7

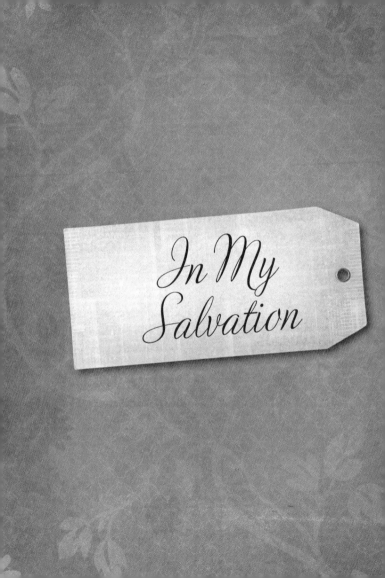

In My
Salvation

Anyone who belongs to Christ has become a new person. The old life is gone; a new life has begun!

2 Corinthians 5:17 NLT

Nothing brings more joy to the human heart than God's salvation, and nothing brings more joy to God's heart than those who receive His amazing gift. We were given the power of choice, and we chose to walk away—but He did not! He paid the price for our sin and redeemed us. Joy is knowing that each of us has been given a second chance to be God's child.

I ask myself,
  Just who am I
That God should send His only Son
That my salvation would be won
Upon a cross by a sinless man
To bring fulfillment
  to God's plan—
For Jesus suffered, bled, and died
That sinners might be sanctified,
And to grant God's children,
  such as I,
Eternal life in that home on high.

Open your heart's door
and let Christ come in,
And He'll give you new life
and free you from sin—
And there is no joy
that can ever compare
With the joy of knowing
you're in God's care.

The Lord is our salvation
And our strength in every fight,
Our redeemer and protector,
Our eternal guiding light. . .
He has promised to sustain us,
He's our refuge from all harms,
And underneath this refuge
Are the everlasting arms.

I am often weak and weary,
  and life is dark and bleak and dreary. . .
But somehow when I realize that He
  who made the sea and skies
And holds the whole world in His hand
  has my small soul in His command,
It gives me strength to try once more to
  somehow reach the heavenly door
Where I will live forevermore
  with friends and loved ones I adore.

*Finally, brothers, whatever is true,
whatever is noble, whatever is right,
whatever is pure, whatever is lovely,
whatever is admirable—if anything is
excellent or praiseworthy—
think about such things.*

Philippians 4:8

Those who believe
in what the Savior said
Will rise in glory
though they be dead...
So Death comes to us
just to open the door
To the kingdom of God
and life evermore.

Step by step we climb day by day
Closer to God with each
    prayer we pray,
For the cry of the heart
    offered in prayer
Becomes just another spiritual stair
In the heavenly staircase leading us to
A beautiful place where we live anew.

Heaven is real

Never give up, for it's worth the climb
To live forever in endless time
Where the soul of man is safe and free
To live and love through <u>eternity</u>.

*And your dear hubby will be
waiting for you. m.*

I am the Way, so just follow Me
Though the way be rough
    and you cannot see. . .
I am the Truth which all men seek,
So heed not false prophets
    or the words that they speak. . .
I am the Life, and I hold the key
That opens the door to eternity. . .
And in this dark world, I am the Light
To the Promised Land where
    there is no night.

He carried the cross to Calvary—
Carried its burden for you and me.
There on the cross He was crucified,
And because He bled and died,
We know that whatever our
*   cross may be,*
It leads to God and eternity.

For all who believe in the risen Lord
Have been assured of this reward,
And death for them is just graduation
To a higher realm of
    wide elevation—
For life on earth is a transient affair,
Just a few brief years
    in which to prepare
For a life that is free
    from pain and tears
Where time is not counted
    by hours or years.

If you are searching to find the way
To life everlasting and eternal day,
With faith in your heart
   take the path that He trod,
For the way of the cross
   is the way to God.

"For God so loved the world that
he gave his one and only Son,
that whoever believes in him shall
not perish but have eternal life."

John 3:16

In Peace

The peace of God, which transcends all understanding, will guard your hearts and your minds in Christ Jesus.

Philippians 4:7

The whole world longs for peace to no avail, because true peace is God's gift. It comes when we relinquish ourselves to Him, when we lay our burdens at His feet, when we invest our faith in His greatness. The heart at peace is a joyful heart, a heart that knows its Creator's love, a heart that knows its future is settled in the arms of God. Open your heart, dear friend, and receive Him—the Prince of Peace.

This brings you a million good
    wishes and more
For the things you cannot
    buy in a store—
Like faith to sustain
    you in times of trial,
A joy-filled heart, and a happy smile,
Contentment, inner peace, and love—
All priceless gifts from God above!

all for you, Fauna, just because
you're His!

May peace and understanding
Give you strength and courage, too,
And may the hours
   and the days ahead
Hold a new hope for you;
For the sorrow that is yours today
Will pass away and then
You'll find the sun of happiness
Will shine for you again.
Take the Savior's loving hand
And do not try to understand—
Just let Him lead you where He will,
Through pastures green
   and waters still.

*"Blessed rather are those who hear
the word of God and obey it."*

Luke 11:28

Lord,

I come to You when day is done
And find You waiting there,
And with Your magic fingertips
The heavy robe of care
Slips from the heart;
And roses bloom,
Because Your presence
Fills the room. *Thank you,*
Lord

While God's almighty power
    is not ours to understand,
We know who holds the future
    and we know who holds our hand—
And to have the steadfast knowledge
    that we never walk alone
And to rest in the assurance
    that our every need is known
Will help dispel our worries,
    and in trusting Him we'll find
Right in the midst of chaos
    God can give us peace of mind.

Though the way ahead seems steep,
Be not afraid for He will keep
Tender watch through night and day,
And He will hear each
  prayer you pray.

If we but had the eyes to see
God's face in every cloud,
If we but had the ears to hear
His voice above the crowd,
We'd find the peace we're seeking,
the kind no man can give—
The peace that comes from knowing
He died so we might live!

After the clouds, the sunshine,
After the winter, the spring,
After the shower, the rainbow,
For life is a changeable thing.
After the night, the morning,
Bidding all darkness cease,
After life's cares and sorrows,
The comfort of sweetness
   and peace.

Kneel in prayer in His presence,
and you'll find no need to speak;
For softly in quiet communion,
God grants you the peace
that you seek. — *How very true!*

When your nervous network
    becomes a tangled mess,
Just close your eyes in silent prayer
    and ask the Lord to bless
Each thought that you are thinking,
    each decision you must make,
As well as every word you speak
    and every step you take—
For only by the grace of God
    can you gain self-control,
And only meditative thoughts
    can restore your peace of soul.

God bless you most abundantly
with joys that never cease,
The joy of knowing that He came
to bring the whole world peace.

Do not be anxious, said our Lord,
Have peace from day to day—
The lilies neither toil nor spin,
Yet none are clothed as they.
The meadowlark with sweetest song
Fears not for bread or nest,
Because he trusts our Father's love
And God knows what is best.

When life becomes a problem
   much too great for us to bear,
Instead of trying to escape,
   let us <u>withdraw</u> in prayer—
For <u>withdrawal</u> <u>means</u> <u>renewal</u>
   if we withdraw to pray
And listen in the quietness
   to hear what God will say. !

So many times He has calmed
or quieted my heart with comfort—

In My
Family

*"A new command I give you: Love one another.
As I have loved you, so you must love one another."*

JOHN 13:34

Ah...family. What greater blessing do we have
here on earth than the sweet voices and familiar
faces of those we love? They are our companions
on the journey of life, adding to our joy. We are
also part of God's family—one of a vast number
of sisters and brothers in the Lord; loving,
laughing, encouraging, and supporting one
another. Our hearts are filled with gratefulness
and praise to our God for His goodness.

In seeking peace for all people
There is only one place to begin,
And that is in each home
    and heart—
For the fortress of peace is <u>within</u>.

Where there is love the heart is light,
Where there is love the day is bright,
Where there is love there is a song
To help when things
    are going wrong. . .
And where the home
    is filled with love
You'll always find God spoken of,
And when a family prays together,
That family also stays together.

Memories to treasure
   are made every day—
Made of family gatherings
   and children as they play.

In my eyes there lies no vision
    but the sight of your dear face.
In my heart there is no feeling
    but the warmth of your embrace.
In my mind there are no thoughts
    but the thoughts of you, my dear.
In my soul, no other longing
    but just to have you near.
All my dreams were built around you,
    and I've come to know it's true—
In my life there is no living
    that is not part of you.

Above all, love each other deeply,
because love covers over a multitude of sins.

1 PETER 4:8

It is sharing and caring,
Giving and forgiving,
Loving and being loved,
Walking hand in hand,
Talking heart to heart,
Seeing through each other's eyes,
Laughing together,
Weeping together,
Praying together,
And always trusting and believing
And thanking God for each other…
For love that is shared
*   is a beautiful thing—*
It enriches the soul
*   and makes the heart sing.*

There's a road I call Remembrance
    where I walk each day with you.
It's a pleasant, happy road, my dear,
    all filled with memories true.
Today it leads me through a spot
    where I can dream awhile,
And in its tranquil peacefulness
    I touch your hand and smile.

There are hills and fields and
    budding trees and stillness
    that's so sweet.
That it seems that this must be
    the place where God and
    humans meet.
I hope we can go back again
    and golden hours renew,
And God go with you always,
    dear, until the day we do.

It takes a mother's kindness
    to forgive us when we err,
To sympathize in trouble
    and bow her head in prayer.
It takes a mother's wisdom
    to recognize our needs
And to give us reassurance
    by her loving words and deeds.

Time cannot destroy the memory

and years can never erase

The tenderness and the beauty of

the love in a mother's face.

And when we think of our mothers,

we draw nearer to God above,

For only God in His greatness

could fashion a mother's love.

A baby is a gift of life
   born of the wonder of love—
A little bit of eternity
   sent from the Father above,
Giving a new dimension to the
   love between husband and wife
And putting an added new
   meaning to the wonder
   and mystery of life.

A wee bit of heaven drifted
    down from above—
A handful of happiness,
    a heart full of love.
The mystery of life so sacred
    and sweet,
The giver of joy so deep
    and complete.
Precious and priceless,
    so lovable, too—
The world's sweetest miracle,
    baby, is you.

Train a child in the way he should go,
and when he is old he will not turn from it.

Proverbs 22:6

Tender little memories
    of some word or deed
Give us strength and courage
    when we are in need.
Blessed little memories
    help to bear the cross
And soften all the bitterness
    of failure and of loss.
Precious little memories
    of little things we've done
Make the very darkest day
    a bright and happy one.

Ten little fingers, ten little toes,
Tiny as a minute, sweet as a rose—
One of life's mysteries,
   which nobody knows,
And one of the miracles
   only God can disclose.

In God's Love

*God is love. Whoever lives in love lives in God,
and God in him.*

1 John 4:16

The Bible says that love is the greatest of all
virtues—and it must be true, for that is where
all others begin and end. It was God's love that
caused Him to create us and His love that bought
us back when sin separated us from Him. It is His
love in our hearts that fuels kindness, gentleness,
meekness, faith, and joy in our lives. God's love
surrounds you, dear friend.

A warm, ready smile or a kind,
    thoughtful deed
Or a hand outstretched
    in an hour of need
Can change our whole outlook
    and make the world bright
Where a minute before
    just nothing seemed right—
It's a wonderful world
    and it always will be
If we keep our eyes open
    and focused to see
The wonderful things
    man is capable of
When he opens his heart
    to God and His love.

Take heart and stand tall
and think who you are,
For God is your Father
and no one can bar
Or keep you from reaching
your desired success,
Or withhold the joy
that is yours to possess.

Dear Fauna,

What more can we ask of our Father
Than to know we are never alone,
That His mercy and love are unfailing,
And He makes all our problems
   His own.— Bless & Praise the Lord!

His love knows no exceptions,
so never feel excluded—
No matter who or what you are,
your name has been included.

You need nothing more than
    God's guidance and love
To ensure the things that you're
    most worthy of...
So trust in His wisdom
    and follow His ways,
And be not concerned
    with the world's empty praise,
But seek first His kingdom,
    and you will possess
The world's greatest riches,
    which is true happiness.

God's love endures forever—
    what a wonderful thing to know
When the tides of life run against
    you and your spirit is downcast
    and low. . .
God's kindness is ever around you,
    always ready to freely impart
Strength to your faltering spirit,
    cheer to your lonely heart.

Delight yourself in the Lord *and he will give you the desires of your heart.*

Psalm 37:4

*Don't doubt for a minute
   that this is not true,
For God loves His children
   and takes care of them, too. . .
And all of His treasures
   are yours to share
If you love Him completely
   and show that you care. . .
And if you walk in His footsteps
   and have faith to believe,
There's nothing you ask for
   that you will not receive.*

No matter what your past has been,
Trust God to understand.
And no matter what your problem is
Just place it in His hand—
For in all of our unloveliness,
This great God loves us still—
He loved us since the world began
And what's more, He always will.

God's love is like an island
    in life's ocean vast and wide—
A peaceful, quiet shelter from
    the restless, rising tide. . .
God's love is like a fortress,
    and we seek protection there
When the waves of tribulation
    seem to drown us in despair. . .
God's love is like a beacon
    burning bright with faith and prayer
And through the changing scenes of life
    we can find a haven there!

We are all God's children
   and He loves us, every one.
He freely and completely
   forgives all that we have done,
Asking only if we're ready
   to go where He leads,
Content that in His wisdom
   He will answer all our needs.

Kings and kingdoms all pass away—
Nothing on earth endures. . .
But the love of God who sent His Son
Is forever and ever yours!

What is love? No words can define it—
It's something so great
    only God could design it.
For love means much more
    than small words can express,
For what we call love is very much less
Than the beauty and depth
    and the true richness of
God's gift to mankind—
    His compassionate love.

Somebody loves you
more than you know,
Somebody goes with you
wherever you go,
Somebody really and truly cares
And lovingly listens
to all of your prayers.
And if you walk in His footsteps
and have faith to believe,
There's nothing you ask for
that you will not receive.

"If you believe, you will receive whatever you ask for in prayer."

MATTHEW 21:22

He promised!

Wait with a heart that is patient
For the goodness of
God to prevail—
For never do prayers
go unanswered,
And His mercy and
love never fail.

In all these things we are more than conquerors through him who loved us.

Romans 8:37

In My Friends

Dear friends, let us continue to love one another,
for love comes from God. Anyone who loves
is a child of God and knows God.

1 John 4:7 nlt

Friends are a priceless gift. Without the
obligation of kin, they choose to be there for
you when skies are fair and when stormy winds
blow. They hold your hand when you are
suffering and share your joy when blessings
flow. Embrace your friends and hold them
close, for they are more precious than silver
or gold. They sparkle more brightly than
diamonds. Treasure them. And strive to
be the best friend you can be to them.

Across the years we've met in dreams
And shared each other's
   hopes and schemes,
We knew a friendship rich and rare
And beauty far beyond compare.
Then you reached out your
   arms for more,
To catch what you were yearning for.
But little did you think or guess
That one can't capture happiness
Because it's unrestrained and free,
Unfettered by reality.

*Who can say just what makes a friend
Or why one heart and another blend?*

Life is like a garden
And friendship like a flower
That blooms and grows in beauty
With the sunshine and the shower.
And in the garden of the heart,
Friendship's flower opens wide
When we shower it with kindness
As our love shines from inside.

Among the great and glorious gifts
    our heavenly Father sends
Is the gift of understanding
    that we find in loving friends,
For it's not money or gifts
    or material things,
But understanding the joy it brings,
That can change this old world
    in wonderful ways
And put goodness and mercy
    back in our days.

Accept one another,
then, just as Christ accepted you,
in order to bring praise to God.

Romans 15:7

In this troubled world
   it's refreshing to find
Someone who still has
   the time to be kind,
Someone who still has
   the faith to believe
That the more you give,
   the more you receive,
Someone who's ready by thought,
   word, or deed
To reach out a hand
   in the hour of need.

The unexpected kindness
    from an unexpected place,
A hand outstretched in friendship,
    a smile on someone's face,
A word of understanding
    spoken in an hour of trial
Are unexpected miracles
    that make life more worthwhile.

We do not know how it happened
in an hour of need
Somebody out of nowhere
proved to be a friend indeed.
For God has many messengers
we fail to recognize,
But He sends them when we need
them for His ways are
wondrously wise!

It's not the things that can be bought that
    are life's richest treasure,
It's just the little heart gifts
    that money cannot measure...
A cheerful smile, a friendly word,
    a sympathetic nod
Are priceless little treasures
    from the storehouse of our God.

Each time you smile,
* you'll find that it's true,*
Somebody, somewhere
* will smile back at you.*
And nothing on earth can make
* life more worthwhile*
Than the sunshine and warmth
* of a beautiful smile.*

Somehow in the generous heart
of loving, faithful friends
The good God in His charity
and wisdom always sends
A sense of understanding
and the power of perception
And mixes these fine qualities
with kindness and affection.

Friends and prayers
   are priceless treasures
Beyond all monetary measures,
And so I say a special prayer
That God will keep you in His care.

I really do care! M.

*"For where your treasure is,
there your heart will be also."*

Matthew 6:21

There is no garden so complete
But roses could make
    the place more sweet.
There is no life so rich and rare
But one more friend
    could enter there.
Like roses in a garden,
    kindness fills the air
With a certain bit of sweetness
    as it touches everywhere.

Nothing on earth can make
    life more worthwhile
Than a true, loyal friend
    and the warmth of a smile,
For, just like a sunbeam
    makes the cloudy days brighter,
The smile of a friend
    makes a heavy heart lighter.

In Daily Living

*"I will see you again and you will rejoice,
and no one will take away your joy."*

John 16:22

God's blessings are all around us, adorning our everyday lives. His constant love and care. His promise to always be with us. The wonders of His creation. We might expect God to bless us when our lives are through—if we have indeed lived virtuous lives. But God blesses us in the here and now, in the course of our daily living. Receive His joy, for your God has made you His own both in this life and the never-ending life to come.

Since fear and dread and worry
  cannot help in any way,
It's much healthier and happier
  to be cheerful every day. . .
And if you'll only try it,
  you will find, without a doubt,
A cheerful attitude's something
  no one should be without.

Happiness is something
we create in our minds—
It's not something you search for
and so seldom find.
It's just waking up and
beginning the day
By counting our blessings
and kneeling to pray.

In the beauty of a snowflake,

Falling softly on the land,

Is the mystery and the miracle

Of God's great, creative hand.

God lives in the beauty
that comes with spring—
The colorful flower,
the birds that sing.

*Give thanks to the L*ORD*, for he is good.*
His love endures forever.

PSALM 136:1

When the heart is cheerful,
   it cannot be filled with fear,
And without fear, the way ahead
   seems more distinct and clear,
And we realize there's nothing
   that we must face alone,
For our heavenly Father loves us,
   and our problems are His own.

Thank You, God, for little things
 that often come our way—
The things we take for granted
 but don't mention when we pray—
The unexpected courtesy,
 the thoughtful, kindly deed—
A hand reached out to help us
 in the time of sudden need.

A little laughter, a little song,
A little teardrop
When things go wrong,
A little calm
And a little strife,
A little loving—
And that is life.

Yesterday's dead,
 tomorrow's unborn,
So there's nothing to fear
 and nothing to mourn,
For it's only the memory
 of things that have been
And expecting tomorrow
 to bring trouble again
That fills my today,
 which God wants to bless,
With uncertain fears
 and borrowed distress.
For all I need live for is this
 one little minute,
For life's here and now,
 and eternity's in it.

God gives us a power
    we so seldom employ,
For we're so unaware
    it is filled with such joy.
The gift that God gives us
    is anticipation,
Which we can fulfill
    with sincere expectation,
For there's power in belief
    when we think we will find
Joy for the heart and peace
    for the mind.
And believing the day
    will bring a surprise
Is not only pleasant
    but surprisingly wise.

If we open the door to let
joy walk through,
When we learn to expect
the best and most, too,
And believing we'll find
a happy surprise
Makes reality out of
a fancied surmise.

Into our lives come many things
to break the dull routine—
The things we had not planned on that
happen unforeseen—
The unexpected little joys that
are scattered on our way,
Success we did not count on
or a rare, fulfilling day.

Let us give ourselves away,

Not just today but every day,

And remember,
   a kind and thoughtful deed

Or a hand outstretched
   in a time of need

Is the rarest of gifts, for it is a part

Not of the purse but a loving heart;

And he who gives of himself
   will find

True joy of heart and peace of mind.

Sometimes when faith is running low
And I cannot fathom why things are so. . .
I walk among the flowers I grow
And learn the answers to all
   I would know. . .
For among my flowers I have come to see
Life's miracle and its mystery,
And standing in silence and reverie,
My faith comes flooding back to me.

Perfume and incense bring joy to the heart,
and the pleasantness of one's friend springs
from his earnest counsel.

PROVERBS 27:9

Thank You for the miracles
    we are much too blind to see,
And give us new awareness
    of our many gifts from Thee,
And help us to remember
    that the key to life and living
Is to make each prayer a prayer of
    thanks and every day Thanksgiving.

Do not be anxious about anything,
but in everything, by prayer and petition,
with thanksgiving, present your requests to God.

Philippians 4:6

Birthdays are a steppingstone
To endless joys as yet unknown—
So fill each day with happy things,
And may your burdens all take wings
And fly away and leave behind
Great joy of heart and peace of mind.

Great is our loss when
  we no longer find
A thankful response
  to things of this kind.
For the joy of enjoying
  and the fullness of living
Are found in the heart
  that is filled with thanksgiving.

America's beloved inspirational poet laureate, **Helen Steiner Rice**, has encouraged millions of people through her beautiful and uplifting verse. Born in Lorain, Ohio, in 1900, Helen was the daughter of a railroad man and an accomplished seamstress and began writing poetry at a young age.

In 1918, Helen began working for a public utilities company and eventually became one of the first female advertising managers and public speakers in the country. In January 1929, she married a wealthy banker named Franklin Rice, who later sank into depression during the Great Depression and eventually committed suicide. Helen later said that her suffering made her sensitive to the pain of others. Her sadness helped her to write some of her most uplifting verses.

Her work for a Cincinnati, Ohio, greeting card company eventually led to her nationwide popularity as a poet when her Christmas card poem "The Priceless Gift of Christmas" was first read on the *Lawrence Welk Show*. Soon Helen had produced several books of her poetry that were a source of inspiration to millions of readers.

Helen died in 1981, leaving a foundation in her name to offer assistance to the needy and the elderly. Now more than twenty-five years after her death, Helen's words still speak powerfully to the hearts of readers about love and comfort, faith and hope, peace and joy.